The Gift of Wisdom

ISBN: 1 86476 179 2

Copyright © Axiom Publishing, 2002.
Unit 2, 1 Union Street, Stepney, South Australia, 5069.
Reprinted in 2004

AXIOM
AUSTRALIA

The Gift of
Wisdom

Character is power; it makes friends,
draws patronage and support and opens the way to wealth,
honour and happiness.

John Howe

There's a fine line between character building and soul destroying.
Colin Hay

To keep your character intact you cannot stoop to filthy acts.
It makes it easier to stoop the next time.

Katharine Hepburn

Getting ahead in a difficult profession requires avid faith in yourself.
You must be able to sustain yourself against staggering blows.
There is no code of conduct to help beginners.
That is why some people with mediocre talent, but with great inner drive,
go much further than people with vastly superior talent.

Sophia Loren

Watch your thoughts; they become words.
Watch your words; they become actions.
Watch your actions; they become habits.
Watch your habits; they become character.
Watch your character; it becomes your destiny.

Frank Outlaw

The depth and strength of a human character are defined
by its moral reserves.
People reveal themselves completely only when they are thrown out of the
customary conditions of their life,
for only then do they have to fall back on their reserves.

Leon Trotsky

Nothing is ever lost by courtesy. It is the cheapest of the pleasures;
costs nothing and conveys much.
It pleases him who gives and; him who receives, and thus, like mercy,
it is twice blessed.

Erastus Wiman

You know the hardest thing about having cerebral palsy and being a
woman? It's plucking your eyebrows.
That's how I originally got pierced ears.

Geri Jewell

The quality of strength lined with tenderness is an unbeatable
combination, as are intelligence and necessity when unblunted by
formal education.

Maya Angelou

The ultimate measure of a man is not where he stands in moments of comfort and convenience, but where he stands at times of challenge and controversy.

Dr. Martin Luther King Jr.

Life is what happens when you are making other plans.

John Lennon

Never doubt that a small group of thoughtful committed citizens can change the world, indeed it is the only thing that ever has.

Margaret Mead, (1901-78)

We don't see things as they are, we see them as we are.
Anais Nin

It is up to us to give ourselves recognition.
If we wait for it to come from others, we feel resentful when it doesn't,
and when it does, we may well reject it.
Bernard Berkowitz

There is a serious defect in the thinking of someone who wants —more
than anything else —to become rich.
As long as they don't have the money, it'll seem like a worthwhile goal.
Once they do, they'll understand how important other things are
—and have always been.
Joseph Brooks

There's a basic human weakness inherent in all people which tempts them to want what they can't have and not what is readily available to them.

Robert J. Ringer

You can buy a person's time; you can buy their physical presence at a given place; you can even buy a measured
number of their skilled muscular motions per hour. But you can not buy enthusiasm... you can not buy loyalty. You can not buy the devotion of hearts, minds, or souls. You must earn these.

Clarence Francis

I feel no need for any other faith than my faith in the kindness on human beings. I am so absorbed in the wonder of earth and the life upon it that I cannot think on heaven and angels.

Perl S. Buck

I try to take one day at a time,
but sometimes several days attack me at once.

Jennifer Unlimited

No iron chain, or outward force of any kind, can ever compel the soul of a person to believe or to disbelieve.

Thomas Carlyle

The most difficult thing in the world is to know how to do a thing and to watch someone else doing it wrong, without commenting.

T. H. White

We judge of man's wisdom by his hope.

Ralph Waldo Emerson

Hope is necessary in every condition. The miseries of poverty, sickness and captivity would, without this comfort, be insupportable.

Samuel Johnson

We love to expect, and when expectation is either disappointed or gratified, we want to be again expecting.
Samuel Johnson

An honest man can never surrender an honest doubt.
Walter Malone

The whole problem with the world is that fools and fanatics are always so certain of themselves, but wiser people so full of doubts.
Bertrand Russell

When in charge ponder.
When in trouble delegate.
When in doubt mumble.

What is compassion? It is not simply a sense of sympathy or caring for the person suffering, not simply a warmth of heart toward the person before you, or a sharp clarity of recognition of their needs and pain, it is also a sustained and practical determination to do whatever is possible and necessary to help alleviate their suffering.

The real test of a man is not how well he plays the role he has invented for himself, but how well he plays the role that destiny assigned to him.

Jan Patocka

The law of harvest is to reap more than you sow.
Sow an act, and you reap a habit. Sow a habit and you reap a character.
Sow a character and you reap a destiny.

James Allen

It's not what's happening to you now or what has happened in your past
that determines who you become. Rather, it's your decisions about what
to focus on, what things mean to you, and what you're going to do about
them that will determine your ultimate destiny.

Anthony Robbins

Loneliness is the most terrible poverty.
Mother Teresa

Nature is at work.. Character and destiny are her handiwork. She gives us love and hate, jealousy and reverence. All that is ours is the power to choose which impulse we shall follow.
David Seabury

We're given a code to live our lives by.
We don't always follow it, but it's still there.
Gary Oldman

I believe that any man's life will be filled with constant and unexpected encouragement, if he makes up his mind to do his level best each day, and as nearly as possible reaching the high water mark of pure and useful living.

Booker T. Washington

To see the world in a grain of sand, and to see heaven in a wild flower, hold infinity in the palm of your hands, and eternity in an hour.

William Blake

Do you know how to digest your food? Do you know how to fill your lungs with air? Do you know how to establish, regulate and direct the metabolism of your body — the assimilation of foodstuff so that it builds muscles, bones and flesh? No, you don't know how consciously, but there is a wisdom within you that does know.

Donald Curtis

To know what is impenetrable to us really exists, manifesting itself as the highest wisdom and the most radiant beauty... this knowledge, this feeling is at the centre of true religiousness.

Albert Einstein

The real art of conversation is not only to say the right thing in the right place but to leave unsaid the wrong thing at the tempting moment.

Dorothy Nevill

A person consists of his faith. Whatever is his faith, even so is he.

Indian proverb

Forgiveness does not change the past, but it does enlarge the future.

Paul Boese

I can believe anything provided it is incredible.
Oscar Wilde

Whatever we have done with our lives makes us what we are when we die.
And everything, absolutely everything, counts..

If a good person does you wrong, act as though you had not noticed it.
They will make note of this and not remain in your debt long.
Johann Wolfgang Von Goethe

A winner rebukes and forgives; a loser is too timid to rebuke and too petty to forgive
Sidney J. Harris

If we could read the secret history of our enemies, we would find in each person's life sorrow and suffering enough to disarm all hostility.
Henry Wadsworth Longfellow

We easily pardon an offense we had part in.
Juoy

He that cannot forgive others,
breaks the bridge over which he himself must pass
if he would ever reach heaven;
for everyone has need to be forgiven.

George Herbert

A wise man will make haste to forgive, because he knows the full value of
time and will not suffer it to pass away in unnecessary pain.

Rambler

To arrive at a just estimate of a renowned man's character one must judge
it by the standards of his time, not ours.

Mark Twain

Do not choose for your friends and familiar acquaintance those that are of an estate or quality too much above yours...You will hereby accustom yourselves to live after their rate in clothes, in habit, and in expenses, whereby you will learn a fashion and rank of life above your degree and estate, which will in the end be your undoing.

Matthew Hale

Man strives for glory, honour, fame, so that all the world may know his name. Amasses wealth by brain and hand. Becomes a power in the land. But when he nears the end of life and looks back over the years of strife. He finds that happiness depends on none of these but love of friends.

As a first approximation, I define "belief" not as the object of believing (a dogma, a program, etc.) but as the subject's investment in a proposition, the act of saying it and considering it as true.

Michel De Certeau

He that will believe only what he can fully comprehend must have a long head or a very short creed.

Charles Caleb Colton

The art of writing is the art of discovering what you believe.

David Hare

To a very large extent men and women are a product of how they define themselves. As a result of a combination of innate ideas and the intimate influences of the culture and environment we grow up in, we come to have beliefs about the nature of being human.

These beliefs penetrate to a very deep level of our psychosomatic systems, our minds and brains, our nervous systems, our endocrine systems, and even our blood and sinews. We act, speak, and think according to these deeply held beliefs and belief systems.

Jeremy W. Hayward

Belief gets in the way of learning.

Robert Heinlein

It's an indulgence to sit in a room and discuss your beliefs as if they were
a juicy piece of gossip.
Lillian Hellman

To be absolutely certain about something,
one must know everything or nothing about it.
Olin Miller

"Stay" is a charming word in a friend's vocabulary.
Louisa May Alcott

You must learn day by day, year by year, to broaden your horizon.
The more things you love, the more you are interested in,
the more you enjoy, the more you are indignant about,
the more you have left when anything happens.

Ethel Barrymore

Why was the human race created?
Or at least why wasn't something creditable created in place of it?
God had His opportunity. He could have made a reputation. But no,
He must commit this grotesque folly — a lark which must have cost
Him a regret or two when He came to think it over and observe effects.

Mark Twain

A kiss is a lovely trick designed by nature to stop speech when words
become superfluous.
Ingrid Bergman

What we need is not the will to believe, but the wish to find out.
Bertrand Russell

When I stand before God at the end of my life,
I would hope that I would not have a single bit of talent left,
and could say, "I used everything you gave me."
Erma Bombeck

I've always believed no matter how many shots I miss,
I'm going to make the next one.
Isiah Thomas

And above all things, never think that you're not good enough yourself.
A man should never think that. My belief is that in life people will take
you at your own reckoning
Anthony Trollope

Things that I felt absolutely sure of but a few years ago, I do not believe
now. This thought makes me see more clearly how foolish it would be to
expect all men to agree with me.
F. D. Van Amburgh

Politeness is the slow poison of collaboration.
Edwin H. Land

Only the brave know how to forgive; it is the most refined and generous
pitch of virtue human nature can arrive at.
Laurence Sterne

Character is the result of two things:
Mental attitude and the way we spend our time.
Elbert Hubbard

Property may be destroyed and money may lose its purchasing power; but, character, health, knowledge and good judgment will always be in demand under all conditions.

Roger Babson

If you don't run your own life, somebody else will.

John Atkinson

There are two ways of meeting difficulties.
You alter the difficulties or you alter yourself to meet them.

Phyllis Bottome

Let us not say, every man is the architect of his own fortune; but let us say, every man is the architect of his own character.

George D. Boardman

There is never a better measure of what a person is than what he does when he is absolutely free to choose.

William M. Bulger

The best index to a person's character is how he treats people who can't do him any good, and how he treats people who can't fight back.

Abigail Van Buren

It takes a great deal of strength and character to apologise quickly out of one's heart rather than out of pity. A person must possess himself and have a deep sense of security in fundamental principles and values in order to genuinely apologise.

Stephen R. Covey

Therefore keep in the midst of life. Do not isolate yourself. Be among men and things, and among troubles, and difficulties, and obstacles.

Henry Drummond

What you possess in the world will be found at the day of your death to belong to someone else. But what you are will be yours forever.

Henry Van Dyke

Prejudices, it is well known,

are most difficult to eradicate from the heart whose soil has never been
loosened or fertilised by education;

they grow there, firm as weeds among rocks.

Charlotte Bronte

Old age and sickness bring out the essential characteristics of a man.

Felix Frankfurter

Any man worth his salt will stick up for what he believes right, but it takes a slightly better man to acknowledge instantly and without reservation that he is in error.

General Peyton C. March

The time which we have at our disposal every day is elastic; the passions that we feel expand it, those that we inspire contract it; and habit fills up what remains.

Marcel Proust

Let the past drift away with the water.

Japanese saying

Besides the noble art of getting things done, there is the noble art of leaving things undone. The wisdom of life consists in the elimination of nonessentials.

Lin Yutang

We should take from the past its fires and not its ashes.

Jean Juares

If spring came but once a century instead of once a year, or burst forth with the sound of an earthquake and not in silence, what wonder and expectation there would be in all hearts to behold the miraculous change.

Henry Wadsworth Longfellow

God, give us grace to accept with serenity the things that cannot be changed, courage to change the things which should be changed, and the wisdom to distinguish one from the other.

Reinhold Niebuhr

If one advances confidently in the direction of his dreams, and endeavours to live the life which he has imagined, he will meet with success unexpected in common hours.

Henry David Thoreau

The civilised man has built a carriage, but has lost the use of his feet. He is supported on crutches, but lacks ...support of his muscle. He has a fine Geneva watch, but he fails the skill to tell the hour by the sun.

Ralph Waldo Emerson

I never think of the future, it comes soon enough.
Albert Einstein

There are only two ways to be quite unprejudiced and impartial.
One is to be completely ignorant.
The other is to be completely indifferent. Bias and prejudice are attitudes
to be kept in hand, not attitudes to be avoided.
Charles P. Curtis

Commandment number one of any truly civilised society is this:
let people be different.
David Grayson

I feel the necessity of deepening the stream of life; I must cultivate privacy. It is very dissipating to be with people too much.

Henry David Thoreau

Great Spirit, help me never to judge another until I have walked in his moccasins.

Sioux Indian Prayer

No one can make you feel inferior, without your consent.

Eleanor Roosevelt

Good people are good because they have come to wisdom through failure. We get very little wisdom from success, you know..... One who doesn't try cannot fail and become wise.

William Saroyan

Look around you and you will agree that the really happy people are those who have broken the chains of procrastination, those who find satisfaction in doing the job at hand.
They are full of eagerness, zest, productivity.
You can be, too.

Norman Vincent Peale

My grandfather once told me
there were two kinds of people:
those who do the work and those who take the credit.
He told me to try to be in the first group;
there was much less competition.

Indira Gandhi

Self-pity is our worst enemy and if we yield to it, we can never do
anything wise in the world.

Helen Keller

The measure of a man's real character is what he would do if he knew he
would never be found out.

Rhomas Macaulay

Nearly all men can stand adversity, but if you want to test a man's character, give him power.

Abraham Lincoln

A man has made at least a start on discovering the meaning of human life when he plants shade trees under which he knows full well he will never sit.

Elton Trueblood

The farther a man knows himself to be from perfection, the nearer he is to it.

Gerard Groote

In meditation, be at ease, be as natural and spacious as possible.
Slip quietly out of the noose of your habitual anxious self,
release all grasping, and relax into your nature.

So long as a man is angry he can't be in the right.
Chinese proverb

Courage is an inner resolution to go forward in spite of obstacles and
frightening situations. We must constantly build dykes of courage to hold
back the flood of fear.
Martin Luther King, Jr.

Anger is never without a reason, but seldom with a good one.
Benjamin Franklin

The entire object of true education is to make people not merely to do
the right things, but to enjoy them.
John Ruskin

The weak can never forgive. Forgiveness is the attribute of the strong...
Hatred can be overcome only by love.
Mahatma Gandhi

A gentleman is one who thinks more of other people's feelings than his own rights; and more of other people's rights than of his own feeling.

Matthew Henry Buckham

A man can stand a lot as long as he can stand himself. He can live without hope, without friends, without books, even without music, as long as he can listen to his own thoughts.

Axel Munthe

Non-violence and truth are inseparable and presuppose one another. There is no god higher than truth.

Mahatma Gandhi

The roots of responsibility run out to the ends of the earth and we can no more isolate our consciences from world issues than we can fence off our oyster beds from the tides of the ocean.

Ralph W. Sockman

The art of being yourself at your best is the art of unfolding your personality into the man you want to be... Be gentle with yourself, learn to love yourself, to forgive yourself, for only as we have the right attitude toward ourselves can we have the right attitude toward others.

Wilfred Peterson

I believe that man will not merely endure: he will prevail. He is immortal,
not because he alone among creatures has an inexhaustible voice, but
because he has a soul, a spirit capable of compassion and sacrifice
and endurance.

William Faulkner

There is a fountain of youth: it is your mind, your talents, the creativity
you bring to your life and the lives of the people you love.
When you learn to tap this source, you will truly have defeated age.

Sophia Loren

Ask not what your country can do for you,
but rather what you can do for your country.

Marcus Tullius Cicero

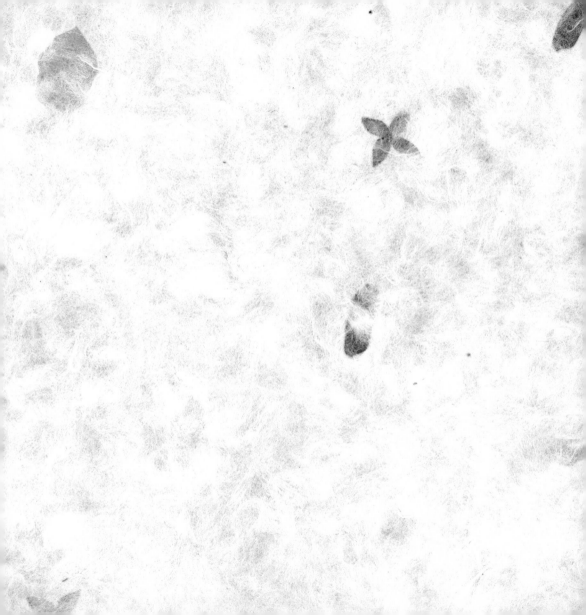